#34

5.00

·THE LITTLE SCENTED LIBRARY·

POT-POURRI

·MALCOLM HILLIER·

SIMON AND SCHUSTER

NEW YORK·LONDON·TORONTO·SYDNEY·TOKYO·SINGAPORE

DK

A DORLING KINDERSLEY BOOK

SIMON AND SCHUSTER
SIMON & SCHUSTER BUILDING, ROCKEFELLER CENTER
1230 AVENUE OF THE AMERICAS, NEW YORK, NY 10020

COPYRIGHT © 1991 DORLING KINDERSLEY LIMITED, LONDON
TEXT © 1991 MALCOLM HILLIER
ALL RIGHTS RESERVED INCLUDING THE RIGHT OF REPRODUCTION IN WHOLE OR IN
PART OF ANY FORM.
FIRST PUBLISHED IN GREAT BRITAIN IN 1991 BY DORLING KINDERSLEY PUBLISHERS LIMITED,
9 HENRIETTA STREET, LONDON WC2E 8PS
PRINTED IN HONG KONG
10 9 8 7 6 5 4 3 2

LIBRARY OF CONGRESS CATALOGING-IN-PUBLICATION DATA
THE LITTLE SCENTED LIBRARY.
P. CM.
INCLUDES INDEX
CONTENTS: LAVENDER / JOANNA SHEEN -- SCENTED GIFTS / VALERIE JANITCH --
POTPOURRI / MALCOLM HILLIER -- ROSES / MALCOLM HILLIER.
ISBN 0-671-73416-4. -- ISBN 0-671-73417-2. -- ISBN 0-671-73415-6. -- ISBN 0-671-73418-0
1. POTPOURRIS (SCENTED FLORAL MIXTURES) 2. AROMATIC PLANTS. 3. FLOWER
ARRANGEMENT. I SHEEN, JOANNA. II. JANITCH, VALERIE. III. HILLIER, MALCOLM.
TT899.4.L68 1991
745.92--DC20   80-19646

ISBN 0-671-73415-6

CONTENTS

3

INTRODUCTION

POTPOURRI IS A FRAGRANT MIX of flower petals, herbs, spices, resins and essential oils, and has been used to perfume rooms and clothes since the times of the ancient Egyptians. The word *potpourri* is French for "rotten pot" and this refers to the moist method of preparation in which fragrant petals are fermented with salt before other scented materials are added for curing. Potpourri can also be made by the simple method of mixing and curing all the dry ingredients together in a bowl.

Many potpourri mixes have as their base either rose petals or lavender, but there are a host of other perfumed ingredients that can be used, including spring mimosa, narcissus, lily-of-the-valley and lilac, and summer peonies, pinks, jasmine and honeysuckle. Scented leaves lend a subtle aroma to potpourri, while spices add an exotic piquancy. Each recipe needs a special fixative, such as orris root, tonka or gum benzoin, to hold its fragile perfume secure and make it last.

The scents of potpourris should never be too strong, just subtle enough to give the rooms in your home a flowery fragrance that appeals to everyone.

FLOWERS

*F*RAGRANT ROSE PETALS and lavender are the flowers most widely used in the making of pot pourri, but other kinds of commonly grown fragrant flowers and leaves can add their own particular perfumes, whether sweet or more reminiscent of the musky smells of the Orient, to your chosen mixtures.

Rosemary *has a sharp, woody, aromatic scent.*

Stock *has a heady and spicy, almost oriental perfume.*

Lily-of-the-valley *is a sweet and distinctive-smelling spring flower.*

Roses *have the best of all perfumes.*

Freesia *has a sweet scent.*

Sweet pea *has a pure perfume.*

Lavender *has an aromatic scent.*

Tobacco plant *has a nutmeg scent.*

Lilies *are extremely spicy.*

Star jasmine *has a stong, sweet scent.*

7

Pot marigold *has a sharp smell.*

Pinks *have a clove perfume.*

Tuberose *has a rich, heavy scent.*

Mock orange *has a heady fragrance.*

Peonies *often have a buttery scent.*

SPICES & FIXATIVES

MANY POTPOURRI MIXES include some spices, and their warm, musky scents add depth to the fragrance of the mix. Fixatives, too, are an important ingredient in potpourri. They absorb and hold the perfume of flower petals, which can be quite fleeting. The most commonly used fixative is ground orris root, which has a scent of violets. But there are many other fixatives you can use, most of which are aromatic and add to the bouquet of a pot-pourri, such as frankincense, gum benzoin, oakmoss and tonka beans. Combine these with fragrant petals, herbs, and scented oils to make your own potpourris.

Star anise smells of licorice.

Citrus peel adds a sharp, piquant tang.

Lavender's newly opened flowers have the strongest scent.

Tonka beans are vanilla-scented and are used to scent tobacco.

Gum benzoin is a tree resin.

Frankincense or olibanum resin is the incense burnt in churches.

Oakmoss has a woody smell.

Cinnamon is finely ground to make a fixative. It combines well with most scented flowers.

Juniper berries have a pine smell when crushed.

Ginger root can be ground or sliced for a spicy scent.

Bay leaves are extremely aromatic.

Chamomile flowers have a tangy scent.

Hawthorn has a sharp smell when crushed.

Cedar cone segments have a strong woody smell.

Vanilla has a lightly spiced, caramel scent.

Cloves can be used for citrus pomanders.

Orris root has a strong, violet scent.

CHOOSING CONTAINERS

POTS WITH COVERS OR PERFORATED COVERS were used for potpourris in the eighteenth and nineteenth centuries, when their scents were much lighter than our present ones and had to be preserved. Nowadays, we can use almost any container that is not too shallow.

LIDDED DISH
An eighteenth-century dish (right) with a cover that helps to preserve perfume.

GLAZED POTS
The vase (top) and two bowls (above), made by the author, are interesting colors for potpourris.

ORIENTAL BOWL

This beautiful Chinese bowl would make the ideal vessel for a potpourri mix containing yellow, blue and orange flowers.

TOBACCO JAR

A lead tobacco jar makes an unusual covered container for potpourri.

STRIKING CONTAINERS

The black and silver covered box (above) was made to contain spices. The contemporary pressed ceramic bowl (right) would be ideal for a blue and pink potpourri mix.

DRY POTPOURRI

To make a dry potpourri, mix together dried, fragrant petals, leaves and seeds with a fixative, such as ground orris root, and essential oils. The quantities of each of the ingredients will vary according to the individual recipes. Place the mixture in a jar, then seal it and store in a dry place at room temperature for about six to eight weeks. Shake the potpourri every day to ensure the ingredients are thoroughly combined.

Lavender

Dried marigolds

Dried rose petals

Cinnamon sticks

Dried strawflowers

Dried mint adds a piquancy to the mix.

Bergamot oil

Ground orris root has a sweet violet scent.

Lavender oil

BASIC DRY POTPOURRI

Rose petals are the usual basis for dry potpourris, but any fragrant petals are suitable. This basic garden mix does not need too many petals of any one flower.

SIMPLE MIX

Mix 1 cup (250 ml) each of dried roses, dried marigolds, dried peonies, and dried lavender. Add $^1/_2$ cup (125 ml) dried strawflowers, and 1 tablespoon each of ground cinnamon, dried mint, and ground orris root. Finally mix in 4 drops each of bergamot and lavender oil.

EXOTIC MIXES

*I*T IS FUN TO EXPERIMENT with making unusual pot-pourris. Most absorbent materials, such as moss, fruit, coral and seed heads, can be used in a mix, as long as there is a fixative in the potpourri to soak up the scents. Try using scents that are non-floral. Clear glass can be an exciting vessel for displaying potpourri as both the top and the sides of the mixture are visible, so you can build patterns.

FRUITY MIX

This glass cube with its stripes of dried flowers, moss and fruits is filled with a fruity mix consisting of 1 cup (250 ml) each of lemon peel, lime peel, and lemon geranium leaves, 1 ground tonka bean, and 4 drops each of apricot oil and lemon oil.

OAKMOSS MIX

This rock pool potpourri (opposite) consists of 3 cups (750 ml) oakmoss, 1 cup (250 ml) each of vetiver and blue delphinium flowers, and 4 drops of sandalwood oil, and is decorated with shells, coral, lotus, love-in-a-mist seed heads and blue delphinium flowers.

FLORAL MIXES

*D*ECORATE THE SURFACES of your potpourri with dried flowers, both to enhance the appearance of the finished mix and to relate it to the colors of the bowl you use for your potpourri.

LAVENDER & ROSE MIX

A large, floral Chinese bowl is filled with a mix of 10 cups (2¹/2 liters) lavender flowers, 1 cup (250 ml) each of ground rosemary and rose buds, 2 cups (500 ml) lemon balm, 2 tablespoons gum benzoin and 10 drops of lavender oil. The top is decorated with small posies of dried flowers tied with raffia.

MARIGOLD MIX

A tangy marigold potpourri in an English delft bowl contains 2 cups (500 ml) marigolds, 1 cup (250 ml) each of hops and sandalwood shavings, and 1 tablespoon each of ground bay leaves and ground nutmeg. The top is decorated with dried marigolds, larkspur hops, and bay leaves.

HEATHER & SAGE MIX

This small, painted Chinese bowl is filled with 3 1/2 cups (750 ml) heather flowers, 2 tablespoons each of ground marjoram and ground sage, 1 tablespoon of ground cinnamon and 3 drops of balsam oil. It is decorated on top with some attractive dried peonies and Jerusalem sage to contrast strongly with the deep blue color of the bowl.

HERB & SPICE MIXES

*S*PECIAL CONTAINERS ARE AN INTEGRAL part of striking potpourris, and relating the two elements is both interesting and fun to do. Color, form and texture need to be considered carefully. Choose containers that either complement or contrast with the color scheme of the potpourri, or that accentuate the texture of the mix. While the basis of the potpourri is most important, it is usually the final decoration – the dried flowers, seeds and leaves, which need not be scented – that makes the ensemble so distinctive to look at.

MARIGOLD & MINT MIX

*Mix 3 1/2 cups (750 ml) marigolds, 1 cup (250 ml)
each of peppermint leaves and tansy flowers, 1
tablespoon ground orris root and 5 drops of
peppermint oil for a striking potpourri (opposite).*

WOODY MIX

*This basket (below)
is crammed with spices,
seeds and
scented oils.*

19

MOIST POTPOURRI

*T*HE MOIST METHOD of producing a potpourri is very simple. Layer partially dried, fragrant petals with coarse salt and stir daily. You can add more petals as they are ready. The final mix must ferment for at least ten days. Add the remainder of the ingredients, seal, and leave for six to eight weeks, shaking daily.

Rose petals

Lime

Dill weed

Lemon verbena leaves

Pink

Brown sugar

Rose oil

Cloves

Gum benzoin

Coarse salt

Carnation oil

ROSE & PINK MIX

Dry 6 cups (1¹/2 liters) rose and pink petals and 2 cups (500 ml) lemon verbena on newspaper or cheesecloth for two or three days. Layer them with 1¹/2 cups (375 ml) coarse salt in a sealed jar and stir each day for ten days. Mix in 3 tablespoons each of dried lime peel and dried dill, 1 tablespoon of cloves, 2 tablespoons each of brown sugar and gum benzoin, and 4 drops each of rose and carnation oils. Store for six to eight weeks, shaking daily.

COUNTRY MIXES

*T*HINKING OF NEW WAYS to use potpourri is a challenge. Country
baskets, with their sympathetic
colors and textures, make attractive
containers for potpourri. Here the rim
of the basket has been decorated with
bunches of herbs and flowers,
attached with mossing wire
and a glue gun.
The basket
holds a
similar pot-
pourri
mixture.

SUMMER FLOWER MIX

Mix together 3 cups (750 ml) rose petals, 3 cups (750 ml) peony petals, 2 cups (500 ml) clove pinks, 1 cup (250 ml) lavender, 1 cup (250 ml) each of rosemary, bay, and marjoram leaves, 2 tablespoons each of sage and cloves, 3 crushed tonka beans and 3 cups (750 ml) coarse salt.

23

COLORFUL MIXES

*B*owls of potpourri can be as beautiful as
flower arrangements. Display them on
a side or low table, in living rooms or
bedrooms. It is best to place them in low light
because bright sunshine will make them fade.

SPRING FLOWER MIX
*A delicate spring mix of 5 cups (1.25 liters) mixed fragrant
narcissus, lilac, lily-of-the-valley, mimosa, jasmine, pansies and
wallflowers, 1 cup (250 ml) coarse salt, 2 tablespoons of ground
orris root, and 4 drops of lily-of-the-valley oil.*

RICH ROSE MIX

A rich, moist potpourri composed of 4 cups (1 liter) fragrant red rose petals, 2 cups (500 ml) clove pinks, ½ cup (125 ml) tuberose, 1 cup (250 ml) coarse salt, 2 tablespoons each of ground cloves, ground ginger, and frankincense, and 4 drops of gardenia oil sits in a bowl edged with striking, dried tropical leaves.

MOIST CLOVER MIX

A basket edged with lavender has a a moist mix of 1 cup (250 ml) clover, 2 cups (500 ml) moss, 1 cup (250 ml) each of Spanish broom and bergamot leaves, 1 tablespoon of nutmeg, 1 cup (250 ml) coarse salt, 1 tablespoon of ground orris root, and 4 drops of honeysuckle oil.

DRIED FLOWERS

*P*OTPOURRI COMBINES well with dried-flower arrangements. I often use potpourri to cover and surround the dry foam in a container of dried flowers, as it adds so much fragrance. If the vase is made of clear glass, you have the added bonus of being able to see the potpourri as well. To achieve this effect, carefully pack the potpourri between the dry foam and the inner surfaces of the glass, building it up slowly and inserting some beautiful silica-gel dried flowers right next to the glass. To position these delicate flowers without actually creasing their petals, try using a long-bladed icing knife and keep checking their position in the vase to see how the finished potpourri mixture is looking.

SCENTED DRIED FLOWERS

A rectangular glass vase is a good shape for this informal arrangement of dried peonies, roses, larkspur, campion, strawflower, wheat, thistles and eucalyptus. I attached dry foam to the base of the vase, leaving a ³/4 in (1 cm) gap around all the sides, which I filled with a fragrant rose potpourri and some decorative dried flowers.

USING CANDLES

*Y*ou can make you own scented candles by melting candle wax, adding one or more essential oils with a few drops of food coloring, and then molding them in a tin with a hole at the bottom through which a waxed wick has been threaded. Or you can choose from a wide range of scented candles available in shops and use one or more in a display that is itself scented. Here a bark-covered bowl is packed with dry foam into which three squat, honey-scented candles are anchored, before other decorations are added. This is an ideal arrangement for a Christmas table.

FESTIVE CANDLES

The center of this festive arrangement is covered with dried moss and pine cones, which are impregnated with pine oil and ground cinnamon. Bundles of cinnamon sticks, blue spruce and tiny, dried, red roses are wired into position among the bark, away from the candles. (For safety's sake, do not leave the lit candles unattended and do not allow them to burn down too low).

29

MAKING A PILLOW

*M*ANY HERBS AND FLOWERS can be used to stuff pillows and cushions. In addition to perfuming a room, they may also help you sleep. Hops, woodruff and rosemary are known for their sleep-inducing properties.

MAKING A SLEEP PILLOW

1 Either make or buy a pillow and stuff it with a mixture of fiberfill and 1 cup (250 ml) scented potpourri.

2 Cut a length of material to cover the pillow, edge the long sides with lace, and sew the short sides together to make a cylinder. Attach ribbon ties to the open sides.

3 Slip the cover over the pillow, and keep it in place by tying the ribbons together into secure and attractive bows.

Soothing Scents
Use any fragrant combinations of soothing herbs and flowers, such as marjoram, thyme, chamomile, roses or lavender, together with spices and a fixative, such as ground orris root, as stuffing for your pillows and cushions. The perfume should not be too strong.

HERB CUSHIONS

*C*USHIONS AND PILLOWS with a delicately scented filling of potpourri and herbs provide another way of scenting rooms. It is important that the cushions have just a hint of fragrance and are not too strongly scented. The desired effect is to make one feel relaxed in the living room, and soothed in the bedroom for a good night's sleep.

SWEET DREAMS

This sleep pillow is filled with 1 cup (250 ml) each of lemon thyme and lavender, 2 cups (500 ml) lemon verbena and 2 drops of lavender oil.

ROSE-SCENTED CHINTZ

This large, glazed chintz cushion
holds a potpourri filling
consisting of 3 cups (750 ml)
fragrant rose petals, the
dried, grated peel of 2
lemons, 1 tablespoon of
ground orris root and
2 drops of lemon oil. If
the perfume of the
potpourri mix begins
to fade over time,
simply add a few
drops of lemon oil to
revive it.

HINT OF HERBS

This smaller chintz cushion
has a mix of 2 cups (500 ml)
mixed dried rosemary, peppermint,
lemon balm, marjoram and basil,
1/2 cup (125 ml) oakmoss and 3
drops of rosemary oil.

MAKING A SACHET

*S*ACHETS CONTAINING FRAGRANT flowers, herbs and spices make beautiful presents and leave the most delicious scent when laid in drawers, especially between sheets and pillow cases. They are simple to make and their scent will last for up to a year.

34

MAKING A SACHET

1 Cut out two squares of fabric. With right sides together, stitch three sides and part of the fourth. Turn and fill the center with potpourri.

2 Stitch along the fourth edge to seal the sachet, then sew lace trimming around all the edges. Overlay this with a length of narrow ribbon in a complementary color, leaving a short piece at one corner.

3 Sew the ribbon along both its edges, around all four sides of the sachet. Neaten the corners as you go, so that the ribbon lies flat. To finish, tie the two ends of the ribbon into a neat, decorative bow.

SACHET FILLINGS

Here are some fragrant fillings for your sachets: pinks, frankincense, and cloves; peonies, lemon balm, grated lemon and coriander; and violets, roses, nutmeg and ground orris root.

SCENTED SACHETS

PLACE FRAGRANT SACHETS in linen cupboards or drawers so they can lend their sweetness to clothes and linens. Many herbs, such as cotton lavender, rosemary and southernwood, make good moth-repellents, and they smell much sweeter than chemical moth balls. Place these herby sachets among your woollens.

HANGING SACHETS

Two pouches that can be hung from a hook contain 1 cup (250 ml) each of rose petals and mint, and 1 tablespoon of ground cloves.

DUAL-PURPOSE SACHET

This sachet can be hung in a cupboard or placed flat in a drawer to deter moths. It is filled with a mix of 1 cup (250 ml) each of southernwood, rosemary and lemon verbena, and 1 ground tonka bean.

MINIATURE CUSHION

This sachet is filled with scented rose petals and dried lavender, and 2 drops of lavender oil.

DRAWER SACHET

This flat sachet is filled with 1 cup (250 ml) fragrant rose petals, and $1/2$ cup (125 ml) each of rose geranium leaves, oakmoss and vetiver.

POMANDERS

*P*OMANDERS, from the French *pomme d'ambre*, were originally fragrant beads of ambergris strung on a necklace or placed in a perforated gold, silver or wooden ball to be worn hanging from a necklace, bracelet or belt. Today, pomanders are usually perforated ceramic spheres filled with pot-pourri, or citrus fruits closely covered with cloves and fixed with orris root and other spices.

ANTIQUE POMANDER
This 19th-century pomander has been carved and pierced from a nut. It unscrews into two halves to hold either beads of ambergris or a fragrant potpourri.

Cloves

Kumquats

Ground orris root

Lime

CITRUS POMANDER
Completely cover an orange or lemon with cloves, then roll it in ground orris root and store in a paper bag for several weeks until it is dry.

ROSE POMANDER

A muslin bag tightly packed with rose potpourri is covered with little dried roses, to form a decorative and perfumed, hanging sphere.

SCENTED FRUIT BASKET

A group of citrus pomanders are displayed in a basket of pot-pourri made from mixed flower petals fragrant with nutmegs, cloves, coriander, cinnamon and myrrh.

Index

Acknowledgments

The author *would like to thank the following people
for their help:* MAY CRISTEA, PETER DAY, MRS P FRANKLYN,
SARAH FRANKLYN, M HANDFORD ANTIQUES, JENNY RAWORTH,
and QUENTIN ROAKE.

Dorling Kindersley *would like to thank* STEVE DOBSON
for his help with photography.

Border illustrations *by Dorothy Tucker.*